Stress Time

Rhythm in conversation

Colin Mortimer

Drawings by Peter Kneebone

Cambridge University Press

Cambridge
London · New York · Melbourne

Published by the Syndics of the Cambridge University Press
The Pitt Building, Trumpington Street, Cambridge CB2 IRP
Bentley House, 200 Euston Road, London NWI 2DB
23 East 57th Street, New York, NY 10022, USA
296 Beaconsfield Parade, Middle Park, Melbourne 3206, Australia

ISBN 0 521 21147 6

First published 1976

Printed in Great Britain at the
University Printing House, Cambridge
(Euan Phillips, University Printer)

For Ruth

Stress Time is based on Professor David Abercrombie's analysis of the rhythm of English. I should like to thank Professor Abercrombie for helpful comments made when I was planning the book. Any errors or inadequacies are, of course, my own responsibility.

Introduction

Stress Time consists of 50 dialogues, suitable for upper-intermediate and advanced learners, in which the main rhythmical patterns of spoken English are presented first individually, then in pairs, then in larger combinations. The dialogues are dramatic, and can be used for listening comprehension at the same time as giving pronunciation practice.

The rhythm of English

English is a 'stress-timed' language. That is to say the beats or *stress pulses* in connected speech follow each other at roughly equal intervals of time:

One	**Two**	**Three**	**Four**

This means that if there are any *unstressed syllables* between stresses, these have to be fitted in without delaying the regular beat of the stress pulses (printed in bold type throughout):

One		**Two**		**Three**		**Four**
One	and	**Two**	and	**Three**	and	**Four**
One	and a	**Two**	and a	**Three**	and a	**Four**
One	and then a	**Two**	and then a	**Three**	and then a	**Four**

The more unstressed syllables there are after a stress, the quicker they must be said in order to 'catch' the next pulse:

●	● ˙	● ˙ ˙	● ˙ ˙ ˙	●
Yes,	**that** was	**pro**bably	**ne**cessary,	**John**

Sometimes a stress pulse is *silent* (indicated by ʌ)

●	●	ʌ	●
Yes	**Yes**	ʌ	**Yes**

5

This *silent stress* may sometimes be followed by some unstressed syllables:

●	● ·	ʌ · · ·	●
Yes,	Peter,	ʌ he was at	**home**

The silent stress can also come at the *beginning* of an utterance:

ʌ · · · ●	● ·
ʌ He was at **home**,	**Peter**

After the basic unit of rhythm of the syllable comes the larger unit of the *foot*. A foot always begins with the stress pulse, in bold type, and takes in everything that comes after it up to the next stress. The foot boundary is indicated by an oblique stroke:

/**Yes,**	/**Peter,**	/ʌ he was at	/ **home**
Foot 1	Foot 2	Foot 3	Foot 4

Presentation

Though variety in presentation is important, the following is a sequence of steps that has worked well as a standard procedure:

1 Students should listen to a dialogue once or twice first. It is essential that the dialogue should be spoken by a good model or models.

2 Students should then answer comprehension questions and possibly re-tell the story to show that they understand it.

3 After this, students should listen again once or twice, and gently beat out the stresses – including silent stresses – either by tapping, or by beating the index finger on the open palm of the other hand.

4 They can next say and beat only the stressed syllables in the first line, keeping these at equal intervals:

    e.g. /**Yes,** / **that**.../**pro**.../**ne**..., /**John**

6

5   Next, they can practise each foot separately, and then pro-
gressively in combination:

/**Yes**
/**that** was

/**Yes,** / **that** was

/**pro**bably
/**Yes,** / **that** was / **pro**bably

/**ne**cessary
/**Yes,** / **that** was / **pro**bably / **ne**cessary

/**John**
/**Yes,** / **that** was / **pro**bably / **ne**cessary, / **John**

6   Listen and repeat whole lines, beating time.

7   Do the whole dialogue tapping the beat, then without tapping,
but with the teacher conducting the beat.

8   Perform the dialogue – possibly memorise it – aiming for
perfection.

9   Old dialogues should be regularly revised.

Silent stress needs to be thought of and 'felt' as a beat. Students
sometimes find it helpful to blow out their breath in a quick puff
on the silent stress beat, or to make a sound such as 'Mm' wher-
ever silent stress occurs:

/ ʌ he was at / **home**
(blow)
(Mm)

These devices help to maintain the beat. They also use up some
breath and thereby perhaps assist the speaker to make any re-
maining syllables in the foot quick and light (students often find
it hard not to put too much emphasis on unstressed syllables
coming at the beginning of an utterance, after silent stress).
Where there is a sequence of silent stresses it is probably best to
count these out either aloud or in a whisper.

7

The recording

All of the dialogues are recorded on cassette. Each dialogue is read twice, first with a tap to indicate the stresses, and then without a tap.

The student should listen to the whole dialogue first *for meaning*, probably using the second reading first. Then the procedure indicated above can be followed using the pause and rewind mechanisms to play individual feet and lines and then the whole dialogue.

Paced reading: Students often find it helpful to read *along with* the tape; to do this kind of paced reading, it may be advisable to turn down the volume of the tape a little.

Rhythmical patterns and combinations

The list opposite specifies what foot pattern or patterns are featured in each dialogue. These patterns are also shown above each dialogue in the text. A large, heavy dot represents a stressed syllable and a small dot represents a non-stressed syllable. Dialogue 9, for instance, is devoted to the single foot pattern/●.. which means that it consists entirely of feet with a stressed syllable followed by two non-stressed syllables, e.g. / **fur**niture. Dialogue 19, on the other hand, features *three* foot types, namely /●, / ʌ and /●. . . This means that this dialogue is exclusively devoted to feet containing:

either   a single stressed syllable only
or   silent stress
or   a stressed syllable followed by three non-stressed syllables, e.g. / **per**manently

It should be noted that the rhythmical specification for each dialogue indicates the types of feet used in that dialogue; it does not necessarily indicate the *order* in which they appear. Thus, for example, Dialogue 28 is devoted to the three foot types /●, /●. . and /●. . . *which can appear in any combination and in any order.*

Italic type is used to indicate emphasis. Syllables in bold italic should therefore be given emphatic stress.

Patterns

1 /•

A /One / One/ One / One.
B /Two / Two / Two / Two.
A /One / One.
B /Two / Two.
A /*Two*?
B /Two.
A /Hm!
B /Thanks.

2 /•

A /Yes / Yes / Yes / Yes.
B /No / No / No / No.
A /Go! / Go!
B /No / No.
A /Yes! / Yes! / Yes! / Yes!
B /No / No / No / No.
A /Oh.

3 / • / ʌ

A   /Where? / Where? / Where? / Where?
B   /There / There / There / There.
A   /When? / ʌ / When?
B   / ʌ / Now / ʌ / Now.
A   / ʌ / Who?
B   / ʌ / You.
A   / ʌ / Me?
B   / ʌ / ʌ / ʌ / You.

4 / • / ʌ

A   /Write!
B   /Right.
A   / ʌ / One / large / loaf.
B   / ʌ / One / ʌ / ʌ / large / ʌ / ʌ / ʌ / loaf.
A   / ʌ / ʌ / ʌ / Plum / jam.
B   / ʌ / ʌ / ʌ / Plum / ʌ / ʌ / ʌ / jam.
A   / ʌ / Right?
B   / ʌ / ʌ / ʌ / Right.
A   / ʌ / ʌ / ʌ / Four/ small / cakes . . .

نوع ماكة

II

5 /●.

A /Jimmy! / Jimmy!
B / Jenny! / Jenny!
A /**Missed** you, / Jimmy!
B /**Missed** you, / Jenny!
A /**Like** me, / Jimmy?
B /**Love** you, / Jenny!

6 /●.

A /**Dinner's** / **rea**dy. / Come and / **get** it.
B /**What's** for / **dinner**?
A /**Some**thing / **special**.
B /**Some**thing / **special**?
A /**Chicken** / **curry**. / **Don't** you / **like** it?
B /**Yes**, I / **love** it. / **What's** for / **pu**dding?
A /**Wait** and / **see**.

7 /●./ʌ

A /Jimmy! / Jimmy!
B /**Coming**! / **Coming**!
A /Jimmy! / ʌ / Jimmy!
B /**Coming**! / ʌ / ʌ / ʌ / **Coming**!
A / ʌ / **Jimmy's** / **coming**./ ʌ / ʌ / ʌ / **Jimmy's** / *come*!

8 /●..

A /**Carolyn**.
B /**Chris**topher.
A /**Where** are my / **spec**tacles?
B /**Here** are your / **spec**tacles.
A /**Where** were you / **hi**ding them?
B /**Hiding** them?
A /**Hiding** them.
B /*I* wasn't / **hi**ding them.
A /**Where's** my new / **pull**over?
B /**Find** it your/**self**.

9 /•..

A   /**Thi**s is the / **fur**niture.
B   /**Isn**'t it / terrible?
A   /**Terr**ible?
B   /**Terr**ible.
A   /**This** is Aunt / **Agatha's** / **fur**niture, / **Marg**ery!
B   /*She* doesn't / **need** it and / **neither** do / *we.*

10 /•../∧

A   /**When** are you / **bring**ing it?
B   /**Sat**urday, / **pro**bably.
A   /**Sat**urday.
B   / ∧ / **Pro**bably. / ∧ / **When** can you / **pay** for it?
A   /**Sat**urday.
B   / ∧ / ∧ / **Sat**urday.
A   / ∧ / **Pro**bably.
B   / ∧ / ∧ / ∧ / **Mm.**

11 / •...

A /Jonathan's an / irritating / fellow, but he's / necessary.
B /Irritating?
A /Irritating.
B /Necessary?
A /Necessary.
B /Certainly he's / *useful*, but I / wonder if he's / *necessary*?

12 / •...

A /Will it be in / January?
B /Possibly in / January, / possibly in / February.
A /February's / difficult, but / January's / possible, I'll / come if it's in / January. / Can't it be in / January?
B /*Probably* in / January.
A /Er.../m...
B /*Certainly* in / January.
A /Admirable.

13 / • ... / ∧

A /Pendlebury! / ∧ / Pendlebury! / ∧ / ∧ / ∧ / PENDLEBURY!!!
B / ∧ / Pendlebury / isn't in the / office on a / Saturday, and –
A /Pendlebury / isn't in the / office on a / Monday and a / Tuesday and a / Wednesday and a / Thursday and a /Friday, and so /Pendlebury's –
B /Fired?
A /Definitely.

14 / • / • .

A /One / single, / please.
B /One / single / where?
A /One / single / home.
B /Where's / home?
A /Where the / train / stops.
B /Twenty / pounds, / please.
A /Twenty / pounds! / Does it / only / stop / once?
B /Only / once. / Why?
A /Oh, / nothing.

15 / • / ∧ / • .

A /No, / Jimmy.
B /Yes, / Jenny.
A /No, / Jimmy. / No.
B / ∧ / Yes, / Jenny. / Yes.
A / ∧ / Jimmy! / ∧ / No, / Jimmy!
B /Jenny. / ∧ / Yes, / Jenny.
A /No! / ∧ / No!! / ∧ / No, / Jimmy! / ∧ / ∧ / ∧ / ∧ / Oh!

16 / • / • . .

A /Well, / Anthony, / **how** was the / **trip**?
B /**Fine,** / Valerie. / **Fine.**
A /**Good.**
B /Valerie, / **when** did you / **buy** that new –
A /**How** do you / like it, my / **love**?
B /**Where** did you / **buy** it my / **love**?
A /Anthony. / **That's** what I / **wanted** to / **tell** you a/**bout.**
B /**What** did it / **cost** me, my / **sweet**?

17 / • / ∧ / • . .

A /Now, / Julia. / Listen to / **me**!
B /Yes, Uncle / Willy, of / *course*.
A / ∧ /Julia –
B /**Yes**?
A /**Oh**! / **This** is a / **difficult** / **thing** to dis/**cuss**!
B /**Why** should you / **want** to dis/**cuss** it at / **all**?
A /**Why**?
B /**Yes.** / ∧ / **Why** don't you / **buy** me a / **whisky** in/**stead**?

16

18 / • / • . . .

A /Vegetables?
B /No / vegetables, / **please.**
A /No / vegetables
B /Just / chicken and a / little of the / pudding over / **there.**
A /Separately.
B /No.
A /Pudding with the / **meat**?
B /Naturally.
A /Certainly, Ma/**dame.**

19 / • / ʌ / • . . .

A /Pendlebury's / coming in a / minute if he / **can.**
B /Coming in a / minute if he / *can*!
A / ʌ / Pendlebury / **seems** to be en/**gaged.**
B /Tell / Pendlebury, / ʌ / tell him from his / **boss,** / ʌ / tell him that he's / **fired!**
A /Permanently?
B /Permanently, / definitely, / positively / **fired!**
A /Poor / Pendlebury.
B /Hah!

20 / • . / • . .

A /Mr / Boddington!
B /Mrs / Bottomley!
A /Why have you / beaten / Billy?
B /Billy's a / nuisance.
A /Mr / Boddington, / please a/pologise!
B /Sorry.
A /Thank you.
B /Sorry, but / Billy's / more than a / nuisance, / Billy's a –
A /Mr / Boddington!!

21 / • . / ∧ / • . .

A   /This is a / **ques**tion for / **Doc**tor / **Carr**ington.

B   /**What's** the / **ques**tion?

A   / ∧ / **Here's** the / **ques**tion. / ∧ / ∧ / **Let's** i/**ma**gine that / *you* are the /**on**ly / **per**son / **left** in the / **world** ex/**cept** for / **one** other / **per**son.

B   / ∧ / **Splen**did. / ∧ / **In**teresting / **ques**tion.

A   /**Who** would you / **choose,** Doctor / **Carr**ington?

B   / ∧ / ∧ / ∧ / ∧ / **Is** my / **wife** in the / **au**dience?

22 / • . / • . . .

A   /**Come** and / **see** us at our / **new** a/**part**ment.

B   /**Where's** your / **new** a/**part**ment? / Is it in a/**no**ther / **dis**trict?

A   /**No,** it's / **ve**ry / **close** to the a/**part**ment that I / **used** to / **live** in. /**Come** and / **see** us.

B   /**How** about to/**morrow**?

A   /**Round** about / **se**ven? We're at / **home** by / **se**ven. / **Come** and have some / **din**ner with us, / **Ja**net.

B   /**John,** you / **haven't** / **ac**tually / **told** me / **yet** who / '**us**' is!

23 / • . / ʌ / • . . .

A /Is it / ʌ / **Ja**nuary?
B /**No**, it's / **Fe**bruary.
A / ʌ / Is it / ʌ / **Mon**day?
B /**No**, it's / **Tues**day.
A /**Is** it / ʌ / **mor**ning?
B /**No**, the / **mid**dle of the / **af**ter/**noo**n, and it'll / **soon** be / **time** for an
   im/**por**tant / **vi**sitor to / **come** and / **see** you – your / **wife** is / **co**ming.
A / ʌ / ʌ / **Bet**ty. / ʌ / ʌ / **That's** her / **na**me – it's / *Betty*.
B / ʌ / **Erm** . . .

24 / • . . / • . . .

A /**Why** was he / **try**ing to em/**ba**rrass me?
B /**Pro**bably he / **wan**ted you to / **no**tice him.
A /**Why** was he / **rude** to me?
B /**Pro**bably he's / **plan**ning to / **ma**rry you.
A /**Why** is he / **tal**king to that / **stu**pid little / **Al**ison?
B /**Why** are you / **let**ting him?

25 /●../∧/●...

A /Certainly. / ∧ / Definitely. / ∧ / ∧ / Definitely. / ∧ / ∧ / **Rea**dy by
/**Jan**uary, / **def**initely. / ∧ / ∧ / **Terr**ibly / **sorr**y a/**bout** the de/**lay**, but
I / pro**mise** de/**liv**ery in / **Jan**uary. / ∧ / ∧ / **Thank** you for / **wait**ing
so/**pat**iently.

B /∧/∧/∧/ **Why** did you / **tell** him you'll de/**liv**er in / **Jan**uary?
/∧/ **Prob**ably it / **won't** be com/**plet**ed by / **Feb**ruary. /∧/ **Prob**ably –

A /**Prob**ably it / **won't** be com/**plet**ed at / **all**.

26 /●/●./●..

A /**Please**, / **where's** the / **hos**pital?

B /**Well**, there are / **two** / **hos**pitals / **here**. / **Which** do you / **want**?

A /**Ei**ther will / **do**.

B /**Well**, the / **Fe**ver / **Hos**pital –

A /**Not** the / **Fe**ver / **Hos**pital.

B /**Did**n't you / **say** that / **ei**ther will / **do**?

A /**Where's** the / **oth**er? / **Quick**ly, / **please**.

B /**Well**, the / *Gen*eral / **Hos**pital –

A /**Yes**, the / *Gen*eral / **Hos**pital.

B /**Now**, / **where's** the / **Gen**eral / **Hos**pital? / **Er**...

27 /●/∧/●./●..

A /**One**, / **two**, / **three**, / **four** / **men**.

B /∧/ **Thir**teen, / **four**teen, / **fif**teen, / **six**teen / **wom**en.

A /∧/ **One** / **man** to / **four** / **wom**en.

B /∧/ **Four** / **wom**en to / **one** / **man**.

A /∧/ **Splen**did i/**dea**!

B /∧/ **Hm**! /∧/ **Terr**ible!

28 / • / • .. / • ...

A   /Mike, / **how** shall I / **send** it to you?

B   /**Give** it to Y/**vonne**.

A   /**Is** she re/**liable**?

B   /**Perfectly** re/**liable** – she'll / **give** it to me.

A   /**After** she's / **read** it I sup/**pose**!

29 / • / ∧ / • .. / • ...

A   /**Yes**. / ∧ / **Certainly**. / ∧ / **Definitely**.

B   / ∧ / ∧ / ∧ / **Ben**... / ∧ / **Isn't** it a / **fact** that you / **say**, / '**Certainly**', / ∧ / '**Definitely**' / ∧ / **each** time you / **talk** to a / **customer**?

A   / ∧ / ∧ / **Possibly**, / **dear**.

B   /**Definitely**, / **dear**.

30 / • / • . / • .. / • ...

A   /**Well**, / **Sammy**, / **when** will you / **do** it for me?

B   /**Will** to/**morrow** / **do**?

A   /**Yes**, to/**morrow** will be / **ad**mirable.

B   /**When** do I / **get** my / **money**?

A   /**When** you've / **done** it, / **Sammy**.

B   /**How** do I / **know** I'll / **get** it?

A   /**How** will I / **know** you've / **done** it? / **You** and / **I** must / **trust** each /**other**, / **Sammy**.

B   /**Mm**. / **Yes**. / **Yes**, I sup/**pose** there's / **no** al/**ternative**.

21

31 / ● / ∧ / ● . / ● . . / ● . . .

A /Oh! / ∧ / **Mar**tin! / ∧ / **Mar**vellous! / ∧ / **Gi**ve it to me!
B / ∧ / **Isn't** it a / **love**ly / **an**imal? / ∧ / **Care**ful, it'll / **bite**!
A /**No**, it / **won't** / **bite** me, it / **knows** I / love it al/**rea**dy.
B /**Yes**, it / **seems** to / **like** you.
A /**Does** it / **like** / *you*?
B / ∧ / **Pos**sibly. / ∧ / **Cer**tainly it / **likes** my / *fingers*!
A / ∧ / ∧ / ∧ / ∧ / **Ouch**!

32 / ∧ . / ●

A / ∧ He/**llo**?
B / ∧ Y/**vonne**? / ∧ It's / **Mike**. / ∧ I'm / **back**. / ∧ / ∧ / ∧ Is / **Sam** /**there**?
A /**No**, / **Mike**. / ∧ / ∧ There's / **just** / **me**.
B / ∧ / ∧ I / **don't** / **trust** / **Sam**. / ∧ O./**K**. ?
A / ∧ O./**K**. / ∧ Good/**bye**, / **Mike**. / ∧ / ∧ / ∧ / ∧ / **Sam**! / ∧ / **Sam**! / ∧ / ∧ / ∧ It's /**Mike**! / ∧ / ∧ / ∧ He's / **back**!

33 /ʌ../•

A   / ʌ Is it / **there**?
B   / ʌ Is it / **where**?
A   / ʌ On the / **chair**.
B   / ʌ On the / **chair**?
A   / ʌ By the / **door**.
B   / ʌ By the / **door**?
A   / ʌ On the / **floor**.
B   / ʌ On the / **floor**?
A   / ʌ On the / **bed**.
B   / ʌ / ʌ / ʌ On your / **head**!

34 /ʌ.../•

A   / ʌ She was a / **nice** / **girl**, / **Mike**.
B   / ʌ She was a / **fool**!
A   / ʌ She was a / **fool**? / **Why**?
B   / ʌ Because she / **lied**.
A   / ʌ And so she / **died**.
B   / ʌ And so she / **died**, / **Sam**.
A   / ʌ / ʌ But you can / **trust** / *me*, / **Mike**. / ʌ / **Mike**! / ʌ / ʌ / **Mike**!!
B   / ʌ / ʌ / ʌ / ʌ / ʌ / ʌ / ʌ You were a / **nice** / **guy**, / **Sam**. / ʌ But...

35 /ʌ./•.

A   / ʌ It's / **winning**! / ʌ / ʌ It's / **winning**!! / ʌ It's / **winning**, / **Willy**!
B   / ʌ / ʌ The / **winner**! / ʌ The / **winner**!!! / ʌ / ʌ **Ter**/**rific**!!!
A   / ʌ / ʌ / ʌ / ʌ / ʌ / ʌ / ʌ It's / **won** me – / ʌ / ʌ / It's / **won** me –
/ ʌ / ʌ / ʌ It's / **won** me – / ʌ a / **hundred** / **dollars**!
B   / ʌ It's / **won** me – / ʌ / ʌ a /*thousand* / **dollars**!
A   / ʌ A / **thousand**? / ʌ But / **didn't** you / **bet** the / **same** a/**mount** as
/*me*?
B   / ʌ I / **didn't**.
A   / ʌ / **Oh**.

23

36 / ʌ . . / • .

A / ʌ There's a / **wo**man. / ʌ In my / **office**. / ʌ And she / **says** she /**wants** to / **see** you.

B / ʌ But I'm / **bu**sy.

A / ʌ Well she / **says** she / **wants** to / **see** you.

B / ʌ But I'm / **bu**sy!

A / ʌ But she's / **sure** you'll / **want** to / **see** her.

B / ʌ Is she / **pret**ty?

A / ʌ In a / **sort** of / **way** she's / **pret**ty. / ʌ But you're / **bu**sy.

B / ʌ In a / **sort** of / **way**, I'm / **bu**sy. / ʌ But per/**haps** I / **ought** to . . .

37 / ʌ . . . / • .

A / ʌ I was at / **Jo**nah's. / ʌ We had a / **par**ty.

B / ʌ You had a / **par**ty.

A / ʌ It was / **love**ly. / ʌ It was a / **love**ly / **par**ty. / ʌ There was a /**love**ly / **crowd** of / **peo**ple. / ʌ It was a / **love**ly / **par**ty. / ʌ But I'm a / **lit**tle / **late** for –

B / ʌ It's in the / **o**ven. / ʌ It was ex/**treme**ly / **nice** at / **se**ven. / ʌ But at e/**le**ven –

A / ʌ It'll be / **love**ly, / **dar**ling. / ʌ It'll be / **love**ly.

38 / ∧ . / • . .

A / ∧ It's / **pro**bably / **some**one for / **Do**rothy.

B / ∧ He's / **kno**cking a/**gain**, Mrs / **Wel**lington. / ∧ I'll / **o**pen the /**cur**tains and / **see** who it – / ∧ Po/**lice**! The po/**lice**! Mrs / **Wel**ling-ton! / ∧ We / **ha**ven't done / **a**nything / **wrong**, Mrs / **Wel**lington. / ∧ They've / **pro**bably / **made** a mis/**take**, and we / **ought** to in/**form** them that – / ∧ / ∧ / ∧ Well, / **where** have you / *gone*, Mrs /**Wel**lington?

39 / ∧ . . / • . .

A / ∧ It's a / **won**derful / **bar**gain, I / **pro**mise you.
 ∧ But it / **seems** a bit / **rus**ty, and / **look** at the / **en**gine, the / **en** –

A / ∧ It's in / **per**fect con/**di**tion, I / **pro**mise you.

B / ∧ / ∧ / ∧ If I'm / **in**terested, / ∧ / ∧ I shall / **bring** my me/**cha**nic to /**look** at it.

A / ∧ / **Er**. . . / ∧ As I / **say**, it's in / **per**fect con/**di**tion but – / ∧ / ∧ / **pro**bably / *this* is more / *suitable*.

B / ∧ / **Mm** / ∧ And in / '**per**fect con/**di**tion'?

A /**Cer**tainly.

25

40 / ʌ ... / ● ..

A   / ʌ He was a / **won**derful / **trea**surer.
B   / ʌ He was a / **mar**vellous / **trea**surer.
A   / ʌ He was con/**si**derate.
B   / ʌ He was a / *gentleman.*
A   / ʌ And he was / **hu**morous.
B   / ʌ He was a / **comical** / **fellow**, and / **none** of us / ever sus/**pected**
     that / **something** pe/**culiar** was / **happening**.
A   / ʌ And that the / **joke** was on / *us*!

41 / ʌ . / ● ...

A   / ʌ She's / **irr**itating!
B   / ʌ In/**fu**riating!
A   / ʌ Un/**rea**sonable!
B   / ʌ Ex/**as**perating!
A   / ʌ An / **irr**itating, / ʌ in/**fu**riating –
B   / ʌ Un/**rea**sonable, / ʌ ex/**as**perating –
A   /**Beau**tiful and –
B   /**Cap**tivating / **wo**man!

42 / ∧ .. / ● ...

A / ∧ Is there / **su**gar in it?

B / ∧ You pre/**fer** it with / **su**gar in it.

A / ∧ Yes, I / **u**sually / **do**, but it's / **re**cently been / **ma**king me a / **bit** /**sick**.

B / ∧ Are you / **com**fortable?

A /**Rea**sonably.

B / ∧ Do you / **think** it'll be / **born** on the e/**le**venth, as you / **said**?

A / ∧ He'll be / **born** on the e/leventh at e/*leven*, as I / **said**. / ∧ / **Punc**tually!

43 / ∧ . / ● / ∧ . / ● .

A / ∧ You /**did**!

B / ∧ I / **didn**'t!

A / ∧ You / **did**!

B / ∧ I / **didn**'t!

A / ∧ You / **did**! / ∧ You / **did**!

B /**No**, I / **didn**'t!

A / ∧ / **Ouch**! / ∧ You / **hit** me!

B / ∧ / ∧ I / **did**!

44 /ʌ./•/•.

A   / ʌ He's / **quite** / **hand**some.

B   / ʌ I / **think** he's / **ugly**.

A   / ʌ He's / **rather** / **clever**.

B   / ʌ He's / **vain**. / ʌ Con/**ceit**ed.

A   / ʌ He's / **rich**.

B   / ʌ He / **knows** it!

A   / ʌ / ʌ / ʌ He / **thinks** you're / **pretty**.

B   / ʌ / ʌ He / **didn't** / *say* that.

A   / ʌ / ʌ He / **did**.

45 / ∧ . / ● / ∧ .. / ● / ● .

A / ∧ Some / **eggs**, / ∧ and a / **small** / **cabbage**.
B / ∧ A / **small** / **cabbage**. / ∧ And the / **eggs**?
   / ∧ A / **dozen**?
A / ∧ Are they / **fresh**?
B / ∧ Are they / **fresh**? / ∧ / ∧ Of / **course** they're / **fresh**.
A / ∧ The / **last** / **egg**s I / **bought**, / ∧ / ∧ they were/ **bad**.
B / ∧ Did you / **buy** them / **here**?
A / ∧ I / **don't** re/**member**. / ∧ / ∧ Per/**haps** I / **did**. / ∧ / ∧ Per/**haps** I
   /**did**n't.
B / ∧ / ∧ / **Take** / *half* a / **dozen**, / **then**.

29

46 / ∧ . / ● . / ∧ . . / ● . . / .

A / ∧ On / **Mon**day, / ∧ you were / **go**ing to / **mend** it.

B / ∧ I / **could**n't, / ∧ I was / **bus**y on / **Mon**day.

A / ∧ Well, / **Pe**ter, / ∧ will you / **do** it this / **even**ing?

B / ∧ I'm / **sor**ry, / ∧ but I'm / **off** to a / **meet**ing. / ∧ I /**pro**mise you, / ∧ I'll re/**pair** it to/**morr**ow. / **Where** are you / **go**ing?

A / ∧ For the / **tools**.

B / **Why**?

A / ∧ For/**get** it. / ∧ / ∧ I'll re/**pair** it my/**self**.

47 / ∧ . / ● . / ∧ . . / ● . . / ● . . .

A / ∧ The / **smell** of it! / ∧ It's the / **smell** of it, / **Gla**dys!

B / ∧ But it's / *nice* if you / **taste** it.

A / ∧ It's the / **smell** of it!

B / ∧ It's / **mar**vellous. / ∧ It's a / **won**derful / **fla**vour. / ∧ / ∧ It was / **ra**ther ex/**pen**sive, / **Char**lie.

A / ∧ You can / **eat** it / **for** me, / **can't** you?

B / ∧ I sup/**pose** I can / **eat** it.

A / ∧ Well en/**joy** it. / ∧ And I'll / **meet** you out/**side**.

48 / ʌ . . / • / ʌ . . . / • .

A   / ʌ It's a / **boy**. / ʌ And it's a / **big** one.

B   / ʌ And my / **wife** ?

A   / ʌ She was a / **mar**vel. / ʌ And she's / **fine**.

B   / ʌ Can I / **see** her ?

A   / ʌ You can / **see** them / **both** at about / **six**.

B   / ʌ Well, I'm ex/**treme**ly / **grate**ful, / **Sister**. / ʌ And I'll / **see** you /**later**. / ʌ / ʌ / ʌ / ʌ I'm a / **father** ! / ʌ And it's a / **boy** ! / ʌ I must /**do** some /**shop**ping / **quick**ly. / ʌ I must / **buy** some / **flow**ers. / ʌ / ʌ And a / **train**.

49 / ʌ . . / • . . / ʌ . . . / • . . .

A   / ʌ And you're / **fond** of him ?

B   / ʌ Well, I'm in / **love** with him.

A   / ʌ You were in / **love** with the /**ar**chitect. / ʌ And the so/**lic**itor. / ʌ And the / **fel**low with the / **wife** and the in/**num**erable / **child**ren.

B   / ʌ But / **this** is / **dif**ferent, I can / **prom**ise you.

A   / ʌ And they were / **hope**less at / **golf**, I re/**mem**ber.

B   / ʌ He's the / **re**gional / **cham**pion.

A   / ʌ / ʌ You see you / **nev**er have a / **sen**se of pro/*portion*, / **Mar**ilyn.

A   / ʌ So in the /**case** of / syllable-/ **timed** / **lang**uages, / ʌ it's the /**sy**llables that are i/**so**chronous. / ʌ But in / **Eng**lish, / ʌ it's the /**sen**tence / **stre**sses that are i/**so**chronous. / ʌ And it's ex**treme**ly im/**por**tant to / **try** to get the / **rhy**thm of the / **language** / **right.** / ʌ / ʌ Any / **ques**tions?

B   Why – is – it – im – por – tant, – and – what – do – you – mean – by – 'i – so – chro – nous'?

A   / ʌ / **Why** is it im/**por**tant, and / **What** do I / **mean** by 'i/**so**chronous'? / ʌ Well, I'll / **tell** you. / ʌ But it'd be a / **pity** to / **change** that ex/**treme**ly/**char**ming pronunci/**a**tion, you / **know**!